Pete the Cat
Five Little Ducks

by James Dean

HARPER

An Imprint of HarperCollinsPublishers

Pete the Cat: Five Little Ducks
Copyright © 2017 by James Dean

www.harpercollinschildrens.com
ISBN 978-0-06-240448-0
Typography by Jeanne Hogle
16 17 18 19 20   SCP   10 9 8 7 6 5 4 3 2 1
❖
First Edition

ive little ducks went out to play,
With one cool cat leading the way.

Pete the Cat said, "Let's splash and swim!"

But only four little ducks jumped in.

Four little ducks went out to play,
With one cool cat leading the way.

Pete the Cat said, "Let's jump and hop!"

But only three little ducks popped up.

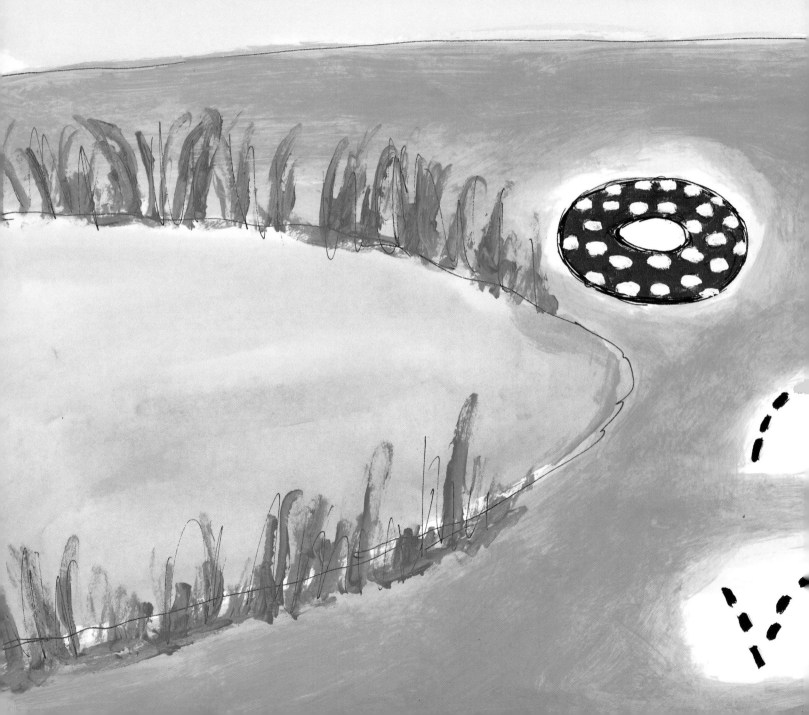

Three little ducks went out to play,
With one cool cat leading the way.

Pete the Cat said, "Let's try the swings."

But only two little ducks flapped their wings.

Two little ducks went out to play,
With one cool cat leading the way.

Pete the Cat said, "Let's run inside."

But only one little duck came by.

One little duck was there to play,
With one cool cat this rainy day.

Pete the Cat said, "It's me and you!"

But that little duck left, too.

Sad Pete the Cat went out to play,
But all of the ducks had gone away.

Pete the Cat said, "Hey, what was that?"

And the five little ducks came running back!

Five little ducks all yelled, "Hooray!"
They made Pete a treat that day.

Pete the Cat said,
"Let's all have fun."

And they played until the day was done!